How You Can enjoy Miracles in Marriage

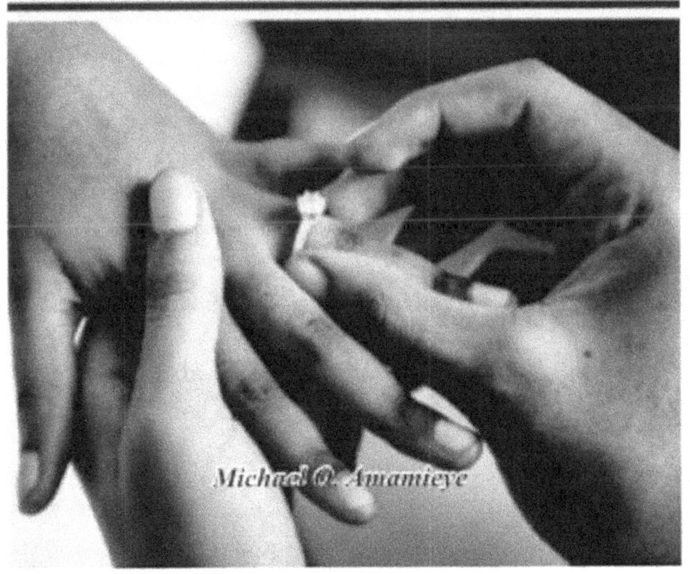

Copyrights © 2014, Michael O. Amamieye

Reprinted 2020

Published by:

Michael Amamieye Word Outreach, International

also known as

Aggressive Faith Ministries,

Plot 13 Walter Akpana Lay Out off 394 Ikwerre Road Mile 5 Rumueprikom

P. O. Box 12378, Port Harcourt, Nigeria.

Phone: +2349018006296, +2348050987377 WhatsApp: +2348036732188

U.S.A.: +19162456157

Website: www.aggressivefaith.org

Email: info@aggressivefaith.org

ISBN: 978-978-51071-2-8

Printed in the Federal Republic of Nigeria

DEDICATION

I dedicate this book to my sweet daughters:

Edwina Aleme

Tracy Nicholas

Mehetabel Favour.

Along with my precious wife, Princess Monivi, they have formed the catalyst for the dramatic changes that have taken place in my life to make me a better man, husband and father. I could not have come this far without them. They make me strong when nothing seems to be working.

TABLE OF CONTENT

PREFACE

The way I met my wife is a miracle. I started praying for a wife many years ago after listening to a message by Rev. Stephen Akinola titled Jezebel On The Trail Of A Preacher. It was fiery. I concluded from that time that if I must make it in life and ministry, I must get it right in my marriage. In order to avoid the Jezebels of my time, I prayed and prayed and prayed.

The time came to make the move and I failed. The first and second ladies I thought were going to be my wife never liked me. It took twelve months in each case to discover that they did not like me over a period of three years. It was heart breaking for me. As in life, when you fall in love, you get injured somehow. So I made up my mind not to fall again.

At the point where I had given up hope was when I met my wife well over two decades ago. I knew she was my wife a few days after our meeting and we got married. Our marriage has not been the best because of our big differences. We had great challenges and storms that have separated us from each other many times. We have failed ourselves many times. But as I write this book, I can tell you without blinking an eye lid that my wife is the best gift that God has given to me. We have both been changed by the word of God. We have both been transformed to become the best of friends today by the things we have suffered.

Apart from education, experience has practical ways of making us learn the lessons of life that eventually shape the course of our lives. What you suffer is a lesson you learn from to become what you eventually end up becoming.

"Though he were a Son, yet learned he obedience by the things which he suffered;

And being made perfect, he became the author of eternal salvation unto all them that obey him."

Heb. 5:8-9.

Jesus became an author after He had learned from the things He suffered. No one should author a book if they have not learned by experience. I have learned by experience and that is why I have authored this book to help many enjoy the miracles in marriage.

This book is what changed my life. That is why I want to put it in the hand of every human being who desires to get married and those who are married. This book will change the way you look at your relationships. It will transform you to become the best that God designed you to become in marriage.

INTRODUCTION

I do not know the historicity of the word marriage. Quite frankly, I don't like that word because if you take out the first three letters and the last three letters to make a sentence, it will be like mar your age. Look at it: MARriAGE. By that, anyone who gets into this relationship without a good understanding is set to mar their age. No wonder we have so many relationships that have been marred as a result of what they called marriage.

Many wounded men and women. Even worse are the results of these bad relationships. The children that have come out of such bad relationships have ended up becoming thieves, robbers, assassins, drunkards, drug users and addicts, etc. Every time you read or hear in the news of violence, abuse, evil against man by man, you can almost trace it to a bad marriage. That is why we must make right the wrongs that bad marriages have caused over the years.

You can imagine the first bad marriage produced the first murderer. Yes, when Adam and Eve broke their relationship with God, the foundation of their marriage was broken. That broken marriage created a son who became a murderer called Cain. Cain killed his brother Abel.

"And Adam knew Eve his wife; and she conceived, and bare Cain, and said, I have gotten a man from the Lord.

And Cain talked with Abel his brother: and it came to pass, when they were in the field, that Cain rose up against Abel his brother, and slew him."

Gen 4:1,8.

From my study, I discovered that the word marriage came from a Hebrew and Greek word that means the same thing: a wedding. In both cases, the marriage emphasizes the ceremony. The Hebrew word means to take away. So marriage may mean to take a woman away from her parents. Before she is taken away, the man has to go through the ceremony of proposing, the proposal has to be accepted. Then, there is the marriage price and other gifts given to bride and bridegroom as well as their parents. After the gifts have been exchanged and accepted, the bridegroom can take the bride away with the benedictions of her family.

There are no prescribed laws that govern the celebration or ceremony of marriage not even in the Bible. Each society or people group have over the years formulated a process leading to the consummation of a man and a woman becoming one flesh as God designed this union to be. In God's plan, it was called the covenant of oneness or the process of becoming one flesh. This is what God called it: one flesh.

"And the Lord God caused a deep sleep to fall upon Adam and he slept: and he took one of his ribs, and closed up the flesh instead thereof;

And the rib, which the Lord God had taken from man, made he a woman, and brought her unto the man.

And Adam said, This is now bone of my bones, and flesh of my flesh: she shall be called Woman, because she was taken out of Man.

Therefore shall a man leave his father and his mother, and shall cleave unto his wife: and they shall be one flesh.

And they were both naked, the man and his wife, and were not ashamed."

Gen. 2:21-25.

While society emphasizes the ceremony, God emphasizes the union. The process of becoming one is a lifetime relationship between a man and a woman who have entered into the covenant of oneness: the covenant of becoming one flesh. This process is initiated by God and consummated by man. God is His wisdom, designed man to be alone without a woman. The same way, a woman is alone without a man. That means without a woman in a man's life, he is alone. Without a man in a woman's life, she is alone.

"Nevertheless, in [the plan of] the Lord and from His point of view woman is not apart from and independent of man, nor is man aloof from and independent of woman."

1 Cor. 11:11. Amplified Version.

The mystery of this union is such that man must discover for himself the bone that connects with his bone, the flesh that connects with his flesh. It is this discovery process that makes any union between a man and a woman either a miracle or a misery. It is a miracle when both of them find joy in each other and the relationship is blessed beyond words. It becomes a misery when both of them are unhappy and unfulfilled in the relationship.

In this book, I want to show you to discover the miracle factor in this union so you can enjoy this union. This union was designed by God for man and woman to enjoy themselves. It was designed by God to keep both of them company as one flesh. As part of this design, they were to find fulfillment in enjoying themselves. From this enjoyment, they were designed by God to exercise dominion by becoming fruitful, increase and subdue the earth.

Chapter One

GOD'S PLAN FOR MARRIAGE

"And God said, Let us make man in our image, after our likeness: and let them have dominion over the fish of the sea, and over the fowl of the air, and over the cattle, and over all the earth, and over every creeping thing that creepeth upon the earth.

So God created man in his own image, in the image of God created he him; male and female created he them.

And God blessed them, and God said unto them, Be fruitful, and multiply, and replenish the earth, and subdue it: and have dominion over the fish of the sea, and over the fowl of the air, and over every living thing that moveth upon the earth."

Gen. 1:26-28.

Everything created has a creator. Nothing created ever existed by itself. Only the creator can decide the design and function of the creature. Without any controversy, man did not just evolve. Man was created. We see the creator of man in the Bible. God thought up man. He formed, framed and fashioned man with a plan that is known only to Him and revealed to man.

"And the Lord God formed man of the dust of the ground, and breathed into his nostrils the breath of life; and man became a living soul."

Gen. 2:7.

God showed us His plan for man from the very concept of man. God designed man to look like Him. The question is: how does God look like? We don't know God except what He reveals to us about Himself. In fact, no one can know God except through the Person of His son Jesus Christ. Jesus said this in Matthew 11:25-27,

"At that time Jesus answered and said, I thank thee, O Father, Lord of heaven and earth, because thou hast hid these things from the wise and prudent, and hast revealed them unto babes.

Even so, Father: for so it seemed good in thy sight.

All things are delivered unto me of my Father: and no man knoweth the Son, but the Father; neither knoweth any man the Father, save the Son, and he to whomsoever the Son will reveal him."

From the above scriptures, you can see a family setting in the Godhead. We can see a Father and the Son. If there is a Father, there has to be a Mother. This is where we have the concept of the TRINITY a triune BEING called God. Although the word trinity is not a Biblical term, however, it can be seen in God and His creation. God is One.

"Hear, O Israel: The Lord our God is one Lord."
Deut. 6:4.

However, He reveals Himself in three personalities. This triune being is called the Godhead.

"Forasmuch then as we are the offspring of God, we ought not to think that the Godhead is like unto gold, or silver, or stone, graven by art and man's device."
Acts 17:29.

God in His wisdom has shown us clearly what the Godhead is by His creation. His creation is basically in three states: solid, liquid and gas. Everything God created can be broken down into these three states.

"For the invisible things of him from the creation of the world are clearly seen, being understood by the things that are made, even his eternal power and Godhead; so that they are without excuse."

Rom. 1:20.

To show us the Godhead, God embodied Himself in a body and that body is called Christ.

"For in him dwelleth all the fulness of the Godhead bodily." Col. 2:9.

So we can see that God has One body but three personalities. God is Spirit.

"God is spirit..." John 4:24. New International Version.

"For there are three that bear record in heaven, the Father, the Word, and the Holy Ghost: and these three are one." 1 John 5:7.

We can see the Godhead consisting of the Father, the Word and the Holy Spirit. That means the trinity consist of a family of the Father, the Son who is the Word and the Holy Spirit who is very likely to be the Mother. These three always agree as one and that is why they can all dwell in one body. It is this same likeness that God wants to demonstrate with man when He made man like Himself. In man, there is the father, the mother and children.

God in His master plan for man wants to replicate this kind of family oneness that exists in heaven here on earth when He designed man. This is why Jesus gave us this prayer topic in His model of prayer when He taught us to pray this daily, ***"Thy kingdom come. Thy will be done in earth, as it is in heaven."*** Matt. 6:10. What is in heaven is what He wants to see on earth. In John 17:11, He prayed, ***"...that they may be one, as we are."*** The oneness that exists in the Godhead has been His plan that it exist here on earth between man and woman.

"The heaven of heavens is for God, but he put us in charge of the earth."

Psa. 115:16. THE MESSAGE Version.

Man was made like God a tripartite being. Man like God is a spirit, he has a soul and he lives in a house called body. As a tripartite personality, he is not a monogamous personality. This accounts for the changes we find in man generally. By design, man is monogamous in a sense because he is a male or a female in one being.

"So God created man in his own image, in the image of God created he him; male and female created he them." Gen. 1:27.

By this design, it takes the covenant of oneness to settle the issue of man's polygamous nature as it were thus making him one. Remember the TRINITY: three Persons in one body. Man also has in him the father, the mother and children. The father part is that male part of man that has the capacity to produce, the female part called the mother and then several other male and female parts called children. It is on this note I agree with the origin of the word marriage which means to take away or to bring out or to mingle. This is so because when God wanted to get the first mother, He took her out of the man's rib.

"And the Lord God caused a deep sleep to fall upon Adam and he slept: and he took one of his ribs, and closed up the flesh instead thereof;

And the rib, which the Lord God had taken from man, made he a woman, and brought her unto the man."

Gen. 2:21-22.

The first mother and female was taken out of the man. *"The first man didn't come from woman, but the first woman came out of man."* 1 Cor. 11:8. The Living Bible. From then, every other male and female have been taken out or brought out of this one man. *"From one man he made every nation of men, that they should inhabit the whole earth; and he determined the times set for them and the exact places where they should live."* Acts 17:26. New International Version.

Through the oneness covenant, every man and woman have been given the divine capacity to create other human beings. No two women can do this. No two men can do this. It is the exclusive power and privilege given to man and women bonding together in this covenant of oneness to be able to create more human beings.

"This is the book of the generations of Adam. In the day that God created man, in the likeness of God made he him;

Male and female created he them; and blessed them, and called their name Adam, in the day when they were created.

And Adam lived an hundred and thirty years, and begat a son in his own likeness, after his image; and called his name Seth."

Gen. 5:1-3.

The word, **generations,** in the above scripture, if you split in two, you will have **gene** and **rations**. The process of human creation begins in God's mind and then planted in a man's bowels in what is called sperm cell carrying twenty three chromosomes. These twenty three chromosomes carries all the information God has programmed into that new being about the sex, skin color, hair type, body format, etc that will make this new being distinct from the father and mother thus creating a new being that never existed. Every human being has a mandate to a great cause to ration the genes they carry in order to perpetuate human existence.

Any arrangement otherwise is a distortion of human existence. The adverse impact of that is the extinction of a generation which is totally opposed to God's plan for man. When men have tried to distort God's original design, they end up creating beings that are less or worse humans. Most children who come out as imbeciles or deformed or evil are products of a distortion of God's original design.

"So also Christ glorified not himself to be made an high priest; but he that said unto him, Thou art my Son, to day have I begotten thee.

As he saith also in another place, Thou art a priest for ever after the order of Melchisedec."

Heb. 5:5-6.

No new human being can become unless they are begotten. The word **begotten** came from a Greek word **gennao** which means to procreate or to regenerate. To procreate means to produce creations after your kind. To regenerate means to generate your kind again or to release the kinds in you after you. Every human has their kinds trapped in their genes which they are under divine mandate to release. No one exists unless they come after the order of someone. The Greek word translated *order* is the word **taxis**, which means a fixed arrangement or succession. It cannot be altered not even by modernization. You are the son or daughter of a man and a woman. You could never be the son or daughter of two men or two women. It is a fixed order no civilization can alter.

Chapter Two

GOD'S PURPOSE FOR MARRIAGE NUMBER ONE

God is a God of purpose. There is no one He has created without a purpose. There is nothing that exists without a purpose.

"To every thing there is a season, and a time to every purpose under the heaven." Eccl. 3:1.

However, when purpose is not known, abuse, misuse, underuse and overuse are inevitable. The covenant of oneness has suffered so much abuse, misuse, underuse and overuse by man. I want to show you three very forceful purposes why God designed this covenant of oneness that we call marriage.

"And the third day there was a marriage in Cana of Galilee; and the mother of Jesus was there:

And both Jesus was called, and his disciples, to the marriage.

And when they wanted wine, the mother of Jesus saith unto him, They have no wine.

Jesus saith unto her, Woman, what have I to do with thee? mine hour is not yet come.

His mother saith unto the servants, Whatsoever he saith unto you, do it.

And there were set there six waterpots of stone, after the manner of the purifying of the Jews, containing two or three firkins apiece.

Jesus saith unto them, Fill the waterpots with water. And they filled them up to the brim.

And he saith unto them, Draw out now, and bear unto the governor of the feast. And they bare it.

When the ruler of the feast had tasted the water that was made wine, and knew not whence it was: (but the servants which drew the water knew;) the governor of the feast called the bridegroom,

And saith unto him, Every man at the beginning doth set forth good wine; and when men have well drunk, then that which is worse: but thou hast kept the good wine until now.

This beginning of miracles did Jesus in Cana of Galilee, and manifested forth his glory; and his disciples believed on him."

John 2:1-11.

Jesus came to redeem man back to God's original plan and purpose. His first miracle will have to be the beginning of human existence: the covenant of oneness. There was a purpose to this been the starting point of His works of miracles. From the above scripture, I want to show you three purposes for marriage by God's design.

PURPOSE NUMBER ONE

God designed marriage to reveal His greatest miracles in human existence. His greatest miracles are not the planetary bodies even though they are humongous and mind blowing. His greatest miracles are not even in nature as we discover them daily. His greatest miracles are not the innumerable company of angels that worship and do His biddings. His greatest miracles are in this covenant of oneness. There are five great miracles you can see and enjoy in this covenant of oneness.

One, Power. This covenant of oneness empowers both male and female. From the concept of God's triune nature, you can see the power of oneness in the Godhead. Their power is in their oneness. So for man to have dominion on earth, man must draw this energy and force from the covenant of oneness. ***"Then God said, "And now we will make human beings; they will be like us and resemble us. They will have power…"*** Gen. 1:26. Good News Translation. Power is the exclusive privilege of the Godhead. They literally have the monopoly of power. Jesus said when He rose from the dead, **"...*All power is given unto me in heaven and in earth.*"** Matt. 28:18.

"Let every soul be subject unto the higher powers. For there is no power but of God: the powers that be are ordained of God.

Whosoever therefore resisteth the power, resisteth the ordinance of God: and they that resist shall receive to themselves damnation."

Rom. 13:1-2.

The power to create a new being that never existed is the greatest of all powers and that is the greatest miracle ever. Man can create practically anything that God can create except a new being that never existed. However, because God made man to look like Him and enjoy what He enjoys, He has empowered man by this covenant of oneness to be able to create new beings. If God does not give it to you, no matter how hard you try, you cannot create a new being. However, you can adopt the ones that others have created. It is still not the same because they don't carry your genetic constitution. They are not your kind. Being akin does not necessarily mean being your kind.

When Rachel was not able to bear children for Jacob, she troubled Jacob one day begging him to give her children or she would die. Jacob asked her, am I in God's stead to give you children? By that he meant, am I God who gives the power to have children? Rachel became smart when she gave her maid to Jacob so she could have children through her even though it is still not the same as having her own.

"And when Rachel saw that she bare Jacob no children, Rachel envied her sister; and said unto Jacob, Give me children, or else I die.

And Jacob's anger was kindled against Rachel: and he said, Am I in God's stead, who hath withheld from thee the fruit of the womb?

And she said, Behold my maid Bilhah, go in unto her; and she shall bear upon my knees that I may also have children by her.

And she gave him Bilhah her handmaid to wife: and Jacob went in unto her.

And Bilhah conceived, and bare Jacob a son.

And Rachel said, God hath judged me, and hath also heard my voice, and hath given me a son: therefore called she his name Dan.

And Bilhah Rachel's maid conceived again, and bare Jacob a second son.

And Rachel said, With great wrestlings have I wrestled with my sister, and I have prevailed: and she called his name Naphtali."

Gen. 30:1-8.

The power of this covenant of oneness is further manifest when you look at Ecclesiastes 4:9-12,

"Two are better than one; because they have a good reward for their labour.

For if they fall, the one will lift up his fellow: but woe to him that is alone when he falleth; for he hath not another to help him up.

Again, if two lie together, then they have heat: but how can one be warm alone?

And if one prevail against him, two shall withstand him; and a threefold cord is not quickly broken."

This covenant empowers both man and woman with good reward. If one is very productive, when you combine both, they become more productive. They are empowered for greater lift and increase. Their lift will be increased in every aspect. Even if one falls, the other will lift up that one. This was what God wanted to see with Adam and Eve. The two of them should not have fallen at the same time. When one fails or falls, it was the divine assignment of the other to lift up his or her fallen partner. Even if they both fall as the scripture says, one of them should lift up the other. The power of this union makes it impossible for failure to be a permanent state. You cannot fail or fall permanently as long as you are in covenant bond with another.

It is worthy to note here that the fail safe proof that God has given man is in this covenant of oneness. That does not rule out failure. It only rules out failure as a state. You can fail or fall or fumble. But you will not stay a failure for too long. If married people know this truth, then, we would not have divorce or separation when one fails or falls or fumbles. You must know it that when you entered this covenant of oneness, you have received the empowerment by God to ensure that when your partner falls or fails or fumbles; it becomes your divine responsibility to lift them up. If you abandon them or separate from them, it is you who failed in your responsibility. You are the failure in that equation. You have the power to lift them up you are just so selfish or arrogant or self righteous or wicked to use it.

This union also provides heat in this relationship. Human beings need heat or energy not just to stay warm in cold times. We all need heat or energy to run the race of life to the end. We need enthusiasm from time to time. We need to be pumped up from day to day. Each day presents us with its own challenge. Sometimes we get depleted that we need refueling. In this covenant of oneness, you will have a fuel partner who fuels you with the courage and confidence to make it. Every day as a couple, you will need each other to speak into your lives. Say a word of courage to weather the storms of life. When you get pumped up daily, you can never lose. Even if you lose, you can win because you have a winner in your life.

You have the power to conquer any and every situation you face in life in this covenant of oneness. That is why God cannot lose because they are one. You cannot lose when you are one with your partner. You can go through hell or high waters together. If you try it alone, you will definitely be burnt or drowned. Together you are guaranteed victory. The Devil knows this and that is why he fights this union with every arsenal he has.

Unfortunately, we human beings don't know so we cooperate with the enemy to destroy the power house that God has given us.

"Live happily with the woman you love through the fleeting days of life, for the wife God gives you is your best reward down here for all your earthly toil."

Eccl. 9:9. The Living Bible.

Two, procreation. The second miracle revealed in this covenant of oneness is the miracle of creation. Creation is a miracle indeed. The ability to create is definitely a miraculous one. There are things you can create all by yourself if you work at it. To create a human being, a new being that never existed, requires the participation of a man and a woman. One reason why the Devil and his demons will forever be jealous of man is this fact. The Devil and his demons cannot create themselves because they are created beings without the capacity to procreate. To procreate means to produce creations after your kind. Produce your kind.

Man has been endowed with this power and privilege. In fact, it is both a command and a blessing to produce your kind. That was why God blessed man when He commanded man to be fruitful. *"And God blessed them, and God said unto them, Be fruitful..."* Gen. 1:28.

"This is the family tree of the human race: When God created the human race, he made it godlike, with a nature akin to God.

He created both male and female and blessed them, the whole human race.

When Adam was 130 years old, he had a son who was just like him, his very spirit and image, and named him Seth."

Gen. 5:1-3. THE MESSAGE.

God designed you to have fruits of your existence. The fruits are proofs that you existed long after you are gone. These fruits are your kind, those that carry your genes and so perpetuate your existence. Apart from your works, your greatest legacy will be the kinds you leave behind.

"Don't you see that children are God's best gift? the fruit of the womb his generous legacy?

Like a warrior's fistful of arrows are the children of a vigorous youth.

Oh, how blessed are you parents, with your quivers full of children! Your enemies don't stand a chance against you; you'll sweep them right off your doorstep."

Psa. 127:3-5. THE MESSAGE.

Three, pleasure. The third miracle revealed in this union is the miracle of pleasure. God wants man to have pleasure called indescribable joy or ecstasy. The height of human pleasure or ecstasy is in this covenant of oneness. When the Bible tells us to, ***"Live joyfully***

with the wife whom thou lovest all the days of the life of thy vanity…" Eccl. 9:9. God means to have indescribable joy and ecstasy. It is the joy that you cannot describe. It is to have this moment regularly that makes a man and a woman connects with each other most times without any plan. This is what makes the chemistry of man and woman relationship a mystery. You cannot understand why you want this joy and ecstasy yet you fight and want to destroy each other. Now I understand. The part that wants this joy will always want this union. The part that always causes the conflicts is the struggle with unseen forces that don't want this union especially when great things are bound to be created from this union.

"Be happy, yes, rejoice in the wife of your youth.

Let her breasts and tender embrace satisfy you. Let her love alone fill you with delight."

Prov. 5:18-19. The Living Bible.

God designed this union to make man happy and joyful. He designed it for man to have and enjoy satisfaction. He designed it for man to experience delight which is the height of human pleasure.

The woman is a blessing to man because she has been empowered by God to make the man happy, joyful, satisfied and delightful. To bring all these to pass, God designed the woman with the components that can accomplish all these. Her breasts and bosoms were not designed for exhibition but for happiness, joy, satisfaction and delight. Any man will crumble before any woman who knows how to use her breasts and bosoms to make a man happy, joyful, satisfied and delighted. It is in making the man happy, joyful, satisfied and delighted that she gets happy, joyful, satisfied and delighted.

"Let thy fountain be blessed: and rejoice with the wife of thy youth."

Prov. 5:18.

The word, *blessed*, here means to empower to produce. The word, *rejoice*, here means to brighten. A woman who knows her powers can empower a man to produce great results. Yes, she can brighten a man's life and world if she knows what she carries. Your breasts and bosoms are powerful parts of your being that can empower any man to succeed and brighten his world. If you want to enjoy life, use what you have to get what you want out of life.

Any man will yield to a woman who demonstrates love to him in ways that delights him. The prostitute knows this and that is why they succeed at their practice. Read Proverbs 6 and 7 and you will be amazed at the success of a prostitute. Now, while we judge her practice, let us learn the principle. She gets empowered by delighting the man. She works to satisfy his fantasy and gets what she wants. She does not judge her client and her client does not judge her. It is business because it brings profit to she and her clients. Learn the principle and practice it in your own marriage. Find out from your spouse what delights him or her without judging them. Just love them for that and see what will happen to both of you.

Before anyone runs around town saying that Michael Amamieye endorses prostitution, let me make a quick disclaimer here. I do not in any way endorse it. And, I do not in any way judge prostitutes. God is the Judge of all of us. Like Jesus, I show mercy on prostitutes because they are beautiful people the Devil just messed up.

"Which of the two did the will of the father? They replied, The first one. Jesus said to them, Truly I tell you, the tax collectors and the harlots will get into the kingdom of heaven before you."

Matt. 21:31. Amplified Version.

Live life to give your partner pleasure and see the amazing miracles this will produce for you. The height of human pleasure is in love making which climaxes in sex. Love making is showing love and affection with a clear mind to make the other person full of joy, satisfaction and happiness. It may not necessarily end up in sex if not we will all be having multiple sexual partners. Sex has to do with the genitals. In this covenant of oneness, you become one flesh with someone else when you have sex with them. Becoming one flesh is only achieved by sex that does not make one ashamed.

"Therefore shall a man leave his father and his mother, and shall cleave unto his wife: and they shall be one flesh.

And they were both naked, the man and his wife, and were not ashamed."

Gen. 2:24-25.

Love making is a need for every human being. Sex is a necessity for every human being in order to ratify the covenant of oneness. Beyond cutting the covenant of oneness, it is a daily necessity to bring the human body to rest from the different activities that goes on in the human body.

The human body is a store house of great activities generating a lot of energies that should find outlets if not it can create conflicts. For instance, it has been discovered that the energy generated in one human being can power a large industrial nation like Japan for two weeks. Now, that is a lot of energy.

Computers need cool environments to function well. So does the human brain. It has been computed that if the human brain was a computer, it will require all the waters from Niagara Falls to cool it. You are a walking power house. If you don't enter into a covenant of oneness where you can find expression of these energies, you are a danger to yourself and the society. No wonder from time to time we hear or read of people who just went crazy killing other innocent people and themselves. Every human being is a potential explosive that is capable of damaging whole nations. Wars have been fought which were started by just one person whose energies were not well directed.

The human body goes through four stages: ACTIVITIES that create CHARGE or electrical or mechanical or chemical energies that must be DISCHARGED until that body find REST. With all these activities going on inside your body, you become charged. Yes, I trust that you know that we are electrical beings as well. There is a lot of heat, energy, electricity generated as a result of the activities going on inside of our bodies daily. Until there is a proper discharge, your body is in danger of either imploding or exploding. When not discharged properly, this implosion or explosion can appear in form of sickness, disease, pain, etc. That is what is called implosion when it is internal. When it becomes explosive, it can manifest in form of anger, rage, violence, murder, etc.

There are two basic outlets for these energies: your mouth or your genitals. You can release through your mouth or through your genitals. Usually both of them drive the entire body to its direction. Until the benefit or damage of this discharge is complete, the body will not rest. But when the body comes to a place of rest, it is always mission accomplished. One reason God gave man the ability to speak is to allow man the opportunity to express this enormous energy with his mouth. The power of life and death are in your mouth.

"A man's belly shall be satisfied with the fruit of his mouth; and with the increase of his lips shall he be filled.

Death and life are in the power of the tongue: and they that love it shall eat the fruit thereof."

Prov. 18:20-21.

Man is the only creation of God's kind with the capacity to create with his mouth just like God does with His words. The Devil and his demons don't really have this power except when men give it to them. You can see another reason why the Devil hates man. The creative power in your mouth is a miracle indeed. Explore it. Enjoy it.

In the covenant of oneness, both man and woman can explore this ability to discharge this enormous energy through explosive sexual encounters. It can be explosive when the benefit is mutual not just for the satisfaction of one partner and you cannot overdo or outgrow it. The benefits are enormous. It has been proven that thirty minutes of uninterrupted sex will make you lose at least two hundred calories. This is a miracle for those struggling with weight issues.

Regular sex strengthens your immune system. It prevents cold. It releases the hormone that helps you to sleep very well for those who have issues with sleep. It releases the hormones that improves your energy level and strengthens vital parts of your body like your bones, heart, etc. It lowers blood pressure and stress level. It makes you malleable because with the different experiments in positioning during sex, your entire body is exercised and toned. No wonder people who have and enjoy sex regularly live younger longer. Mutually beneficial sex frees both man and woman from shame to just be you without any restraint. I love this.

Four, pairing. Is it not a wonder in technology that you can transfer files from one phone to another just by pairing them using Bluetooth? There is no connection in terms of cords or lines between the two phones, yet when they are paired, there will be communication. The miracle of this covenant of oneness is just like that. Two alone people become one thus freeing themselves from being alone. That is amazing. It is a miracle.

"And the Lord God said, It is not good that the man should be alone; I will make him an help meet for him."

Gen. 2:18.

It is not to man's benefit or good to be alone. What is not good is in bad shape and state. It is bad to be alone. In fact, the Hebrew word for *alone* here is bad. It means a part or branch of a body or tree that has been separated. You can see why it is bad when a branch is cut off from the tree that supplies its nutrients. In no distant time that branch will dry up and die. That is exactly what happens to you when you are alone. You are a branch or a part of a tree that is supposed to supply you the needed nutrients to grow. Jesus said it this way,

"I am the true vine, and my Father is the husbandman.

Every branch in me that beareth not fruit he taketh away: and every branch that beareth fruit, he purgeth it, that it may bring forth more fruit.

Now ye are clean through the word which I have spoken unto you.

Abide in me, and I in you. As the branch cannot bear fruit of itself, except it abide in the vine; no more can ye, except ye abide in me.

I am the vine, ye are the branches: He that abideth in me, and I in him, the same bringeth forth much fruit: for without me ye can do nothing.

If a man abide not in me, he is cast forth as a branch, and is withered; and men gather them, and cast them into the fire, and they are burned."

John 15:1-6.

Look at what happens to the one who is alone. He cannot bear fruit. No man or woman can bear fruit by themselves. When you cannot bear fruit, God Himself will purge you from the vine. He cuts you from the tree. You will live and die a lonely human being. The one who is alone does not have someone speak into their lives. It is the spoken words from another that makes us clean. You cannot become all you were designed by God alone. You will require the contribution and participation of others to become.

Anyone who brags of being self made is too ignorant of the dynamics of life or they are too arrogant to acknowledge those God planted around them to become. How can somebody ever claim to be self made as if they came here all by themselves? You came here because of the contributions of your parents, grandparents, teachers, etc. The clothes you wear were made by someone. They were transported to you by someone. The food you eat were grown by someone and transported to you by someone. The books you read were written by several people. So how can you be self made? What did you make yourself that made you self made?

If your parents did not contribute to your success that itself may be the reason you succeeded. If your spouse betrayed you and today you are better off than what you used to be, that betrayal contributed in your determination to discover your true worth. Not every motivation for success is monetary or solidarity based. You can be motivated by anyone even when they don't matter to you. Yet, to a great extent they have contributed to making you become what you are today.

We are all the result of so many people's contributions. Your father gave you his genes that created your uniqueness. Your mother carried you in her womb that made your composition a reality. Can you imagine how they even got all these to give to you? It is a long line of investments from your ancestors. You are what you are because they gave.

For you to finish well, God gives you a man or a woman to be your covenant partner for life. This covenant of oneness will forever destroy your life time of being alone. You can enjoy the miracles of being one with another thus enjoy life together.

Five, protection. This covenant of oneness provides a miracle of protection for both man and woman. This covenant of oneness provides covering for both the man and woman in the union.

"But I would have you know, that the head of every man is Christ; and the head of the woman is the man; and the head of Christ is God."

1 Cor. 11:3.

The word, ***head***, here has to do with authority and direction. Every human being works with an authority that has been given them and that is why they do what they do per time. It is this authority that protects them from harassment and humiliation. The questions you will always be asked are, ***"By what authority doest thou these things? and who gave thee this authority?"*** Matt. 21:23.

No one can carry a gun or any other weapon of war without any authorization. Even if you are in the armed forces or police or any other uniformed agencies, if you are not authorized by a superior officer, you can end up humiliated and harassed. This covenant of oneness provides for both man and woman the authority and direction they need to enjoy life. That is why when a man is married, he is free from harassment from other women even though this does not safe guard him from falling. The same way, a woman is free from harassment from other men even though this does not safe guard her from falling. The authorization is in the fact that both of them can join forces that can beat any odds and they can succeed together. Yes, even if one falls or both of them fall, they can get back up. There is this power vested in this union that can keep both of them together even when the whole world is against them. They can both find security and safety in each other. That is protection and it is a miracle.

Chapter Three

GOD'S PURPOSE NUMBER TWO

God designed this covenant of oneness to reveal His glorious nature. ***"...God's glory is man made in his image, and man's glory is the woman."*** 1 Cor. 11:7. The Living Bible. It is a mystery that the Godhead, the Trinity, is captured in the image of God. Three immeasurable beings compressed into one body that is never dying, never ending. In fact, He is one indescribable body: His image. This is a mystery that no human mind can comprehend. No finite being can comprehend an infinite being. A five by five box cannot contain a ten by ten object. The box will have to be crushed. Any attempt to understand God by man is in futility because it will mess up man's mind. You can't imagine God no matter how hard you try.

"And without controversy great is the mystery of godliness: God was manifest in the flesh, justified in the Spirit, seen of angels, preached unto the Gentiles, believed on in the world, received up into glory."

1 Tim. 3:16.

Can you imagine that it is from that same image that man was formed and framed? This is why you cannot understand yourself sometimes. This is why you cannot claim to know any human being totally. Yes, you may know aspects of them. Like God, man is indescribable to some extent. In fact, we only know in parts. All knowledge is the monopoly of God. That is why He is Omniscient. Part knowledge is our heritage as off-springs of God. It is more like each one is just an infinitesimal part of God's whole being and knowledge.

"For our knowledge is fragmentary (incomplete and imperfect), and our prophecy (our teaching) is fragmentary (incomplete and imperfect)."

1 Cor. 13:9. Amplified Version.

Consider this: you are on a journey to discover God by discovering yourself, your spouse and your world. Marriage provides you and me the immediate environment for this life time discovery. It is a discovery of the triune nature of God which we find in marriage. This triune nature of God, the man and the woman: three beings become one. This oneness is manifested when the man and woman loves each other. This love which only God is and has, He shares in the hearts of both man and woman for each other. It is this love that drives them in search for each other until they find themselves. Can you imagine the chemistry that goes on when a man finds his true love? You had better experience it than imagine it. It is indescribable. It is magnetic. It is out of this world. It can just make you feel like you are special. Of course, you are special. That love is glorious and it is only God who is love can share that in human hearts because He made man like Himself.

"He that loveth not knoweth not God; for God is love." 1 John 4:8.

*"**And we have known and believed the love that God hath to us. God is love; and he that dwelleth in love dwelleth in God, and God in him.**"*

1 John 4:16.

In demonstrating this love to man, God shows us what He can do, give and even subject Himself just to show man He is love. He loves man so much that when He designed man, He made adequate provision for man's sustenance, satisfaction and redemption. At your own time, read Genesis chapter two for yourself. You will see that God built a Garden called Eden for man. This Garden was well watered. It had four streams of income to cover the four sides of man. Man had no need except for fellowship and friendship with God. That is love at work. That is what God designed the marriage to be for man and woman: a Garden of Delight. A place where all you need will be adequately supplied. It is a place where you will have no need for anything else but friendship and fellowship with your partner and God.

Even when man rebelled against God's instruction in Genesis three, God came after the man. Did He not know that man had disobeyed Him? He knew but He wanted fellowship with man. He came after man. This is what God designed marriage to be such that even when one partner has rebelled against the other in any way, you can still go after your partner with love for fellowship and friendship. This is glorious. How many people who have been hurt by their love partner can go after them in this age and time when divorce rate is more than weddings conducted?

God in His love can go to any extent and do anything just for man. The height of His love for man is dying for man. Now, you must know that God is never dying and never ending. If He does not have the capacity to die and that can be the only proof for His love for man, God is willing to die for man. This is the greatest demonstration of His love. God who cannot die chose to die in order to show man His love.

"Hereby perceive we the love of God, because he laid down his life for us: and we ought to lay down our lives for the brethren."

1 John 3:16.

The highest demonstration of His love for man was God laying down His life for man. The never dying God had to die in order to redeem man back to Himself. In this demonstration, God showed man what he can do for the woman he loves. Eve was deceived to eat the fruit that God commanded man not to eat. Seeing his wife had eaten of the fruit he was commanded not to eat and knowing the consequence, man demonstrated his love for his woman by eating of the same fruit so both of them died together. One would not be separated from the other except by death. This does not sound logical when you read it. However, if you were to watch a movie of it, you will appreciate the sense in it. It is a compelling movie of the strong bond of love whose end would only be sensible if both of them had died together. This can change the trajectory of human existence if two people who love each other would rather die together than allow internal or external forces separate or divorce them. There would probably be no event like divorce in human history.

It would be beautiful to see how life plays out for a man and his wife who no matter what comes their ways are determined to stick with each other in love until they no longer exist. That sounds like a fantastic dream. But it can become a reality if we love each other to the extent like God we would rather die for each other than to lose fellowship and friendship with each other. It is no longer the Romeo and Juliet myth. It can become the life style we choose from now on.

What a glorious life to live happily ever after in spite of all the challenges of life! This is what God intends for you and your partner in marriage. It is His glory which is the man living with and enjoying his glory which is the woman. No greater joy and honor will you have when this relationship is your reality. That is why the Bible says, *"Marriage is honourable in all..."* Heb. 13:4. Yes, there is honor, dignity, glory and splendor in marriage. It can bestow this honor and glory in all aspects of your life. Man is no good, no glory, without a woman because the woman is the glory of the man.

"Men were created to be like God and to bring honor to God. This means that a man should not wear anything on his head. Women were created to bring honor to men.

It was the woman who was made from a man, and not the man who was made from a woman.

He wasn't created for her. She was created for him.

And so, because of this, and also because of the angels, a woman ought to wear something on her head, as a sign of her authority.

*As far as the Lord is concerned, men and women
need each other.*

*It is true that the first woman came from a man, but
all other men have been given birth by women. Yet
God is the one who created everything."*

1 Cor. 11:7-12. Contemporary English Version.

Chapter Four

GOD'S PURPOSE NUMBER THREE

God designed marriage to reveal man's best. From the concept of the creation of man in Genesis 1:26-28, you can see that man was designed to be male and female in order to have and exercise dominion as well as the rich blessings of fruitfulness, increase and others.

"God spoke: "Let us make human beings in our image, make them reflecting our nature so they can be responsible for the fish in the sea, the birds in the air, the cattle, And, yes, Earth itself, and every animal that moves on the face of Earth."

God created human beings; he created them godlike, Reflecting God's nature. He created them male and female.

God blessed them: "Prosper! Reproduce! Fill Earth! Take charge! Be responsible for fish in the sea and birds in the air, for every living thing that moves on the face of Earth.""

Gen. 1:26-28. THE MESSAGE Version.

Man and woman were created by God to look like God by looking at God. Your best as the God kind can only come out when your eyes are on God. This is based on the law of reflection which says that for specula reflection (reflections that are produced by light and sound) the angle at which the wave is incident on the surface equals the angle at which it is reflected. Mirrors exhibit specula reflection. Reflection is the return of light or sound waves from a surface. Based on this law, you can produce an image when an incident ray falls on a mirror to produce a reflected ray of which both of them are equal.

You can now understand why a man who is looking at God can reflect God in his life. You can also understand why the woman becomes a reflection of the man. She becomes either what he is or what he is not. If the woman is good, it is the reflection of the good part of the man. If she is bad, it is the reflection of the bad part of the man. Yes, whatever the woman becomes is what the man reflected. She is the bone of his bone and flesh of his flesh.

""This is it!" Adam exclaimed. "She is part of my own bone and flesh! Her name is 'woman' because she was taken out of a man.""

Gen. 2:23. The Living Bible.

Before you write off your partner as a bad person, consider the fact that he or she is a reflection of you. He or she is who are not courageous to be. He or she is who you would have been otherwise. If he is an adulterer, then, that is what you would have been if you had the courage to act it. By the way, it does not take courage to practice sin. It just takes being a sinner. So that is their being showing up in your face. The question is: now that you have discovered your other side, what will you do about it? It is your answer to this question that brings out your bad or best self. If you are bad yourself, you will throw away the bad water with the baby in it. If you are really good like you claim, you will wash the baby and throw away the bad water.

Marriage is a making process for both man and woman. Both of them are being made to look like God by looking at God. Always remember that the goal is to look like God: the image of God. God is His triune being as One who wants to show up in your marriage. He wants to see what you will do with what you have by looking at Him. What did God do? In order to get a bride that was His image, He became the Bridegroom. Bridegroom. That is not just a title. It is a responsibility. It is work. It is the work of grooming the bride in order to present her to him a glorious bride not having spot or wrinkle or blemish. This is a life time assignment.

*"Wives, submit yourselves unto your own husbands,
as unto the Lord.*

*For the husband is the head of the wife, even as
Christ is the head of the church: and he is the saviour
of the body.*

*Therefore as the church is subject unto Christ, so let
the wives be to their own husbands in every thing.*

*Husbands, love your wives, even as Christ also loved
the church, and gave himself for it;*

*That he might sanctify and cleanse it with the
washing of water by the word,*

*That he might present it to himself a glorious church,
not having spot, or wrinkle, or any such thing; but
that it should be holy and without blemish.*

*So ought men to love their wives as their own bodies.
He that loveth his wife loveth himself.*

*For no man ever yet hated his own flesh; but
nourisheth and cherisheth it, even as the Lord the
church:*

For we are members of his body, of his flesh, and of his bones.

For this cause shall a man leave his father and mother, and shall be joined unto his wife, and they two shall be one flesh.

This is a great mystery: but I speak concerning Christ and the church.

Nevertheless let every one of you in particular so love his wife even as himself; and the wife see that she reverence her husband."

Eph. 5:22-33.

How do you groom your partner? If you want the best out of your partner then you must work at grooming them. These are simple steps to follow to groom your partner just like God did for man.

One, see your partner for who they really are. Your reactions or actions are not you. To groom someone to become what we want to see them become we must first recognize them for who they really are. He or she may look nasty and troublesome but inside is a lovely human being who just wants to love you only if you can show them some love. See him for who he is and not what he has done. See her for who she is and not what people say or what you have seen that she has said or done. If you can see the real human being begging for love, your treatment will be different.

Two, give yourself to her. Every woman wants her man to be for him when she needs him. The same way, every man wants his woman to be for him when he needs her. At such moments, give yourself totally. Do not hold back a part of you. You will get the best out of your partner when you can give your best. It is based on the law of sowing and reaping. What you sow is what you reap. If you sow oranges, you will reap oranges. Don't expect to reap mango when what you sowed was pepper. Sow yourself, your time, your talent, your treasure into your partner and you will reap the same in several measures. Yes, there will be moments when each of you want to be by yourself, let it be based on understanding and consent.

Three, work on yourself as if you are working on your partner. The work part is where a lot of people don't want to do and that is why relationships suffer breakdown. Marriage is made in heaven but we are responsible for the maintenance work. William L. Coleman in his book, What Makes A Marriage Last, wrote, *'Couples who do not expect to work at their relationship often have the roughest ride on the back roads of matrimony.'*

Alan Loy McGinnis in his book, The Power of Optimism wrote, *'In physics, the law of entropy says that all systems, left unattended, will run down. Unless new energy is pumped in, any organism will disintegrate. Entropy is at work in marriages. A marriage will not continue to be good simply because two people love each other, are compatible and get off to a fine start. To the contrary, marriages left to their own devices tend to wear out, break down, and ultimately disintegrate. This is the law of entropy. So to* keep our relationships working, we must constantly pump new energy into them.'

Look at the work you must do daily: save your partner. You are both saviors of each other just like Christ is the Savior of His bride. Save your bride. Save your groom. All sinners need the Savior. That means your partner is a sinner just like you. Yes, Christ has saved you when you surrendered your life to Him. Daily, you will need to be saved from one fall to another. If Adam knew this, he could have saved his wife when she ate of the fruit that God told them not to eat of. You will need each other daily to save each other from falling into one trap set by those who hate you.

The work is enormous. Another work is washing each other with your words daily. Washing is the process of cleaning, bathing, rinsing in order to make clean. Why do you bath and brush your mouth on a daily basis? So you can be clean and fresh. Is it not so? Can you try going for several days without having a bath and brushing your mouth? Just try it and see if you will like yourself. Now, your partner is just like that. They need daily washing. It is your job to wash them daily with your words. The words you speak over them will either wash them or smear them. If you want to see the best in your partner, wash them with the best and you will see the best. It takes a man to make a woman. It takes a woman to make a man. The same way to destroy a man, any man, all it takes is a woman. To destroy any woman, all it takes is a man.

A PRAYER FOR YOUR MARRIAGE AND PARTNER

Lord, I thank you for designing marriage for me. According to Your word, it is honorable. I believe in Your word. I believe in my partner ______________. I believe and declare that we are ONE - bone of my bone, flesh of my flesh. My marriage is blessed. My partner is the best gift You have given me. My partner is a blessing to me. And, I am a blessing to my partner.

Lord Jesus, You are the Lord of my marriage. You are my Lord and Master. You are the Lord of my partner and our marriage. Because You are the Lord of our union, we are one. We are a threefold cord that cannot be broken. Nothing on earth can break us. No human being on earth can come between us. I stand on God's word to declare that we are blessed in the name of Jesus Christ our Lord and Master.

Lord Jesus, I declare that my partner loves me and I love my partner. We are in love with each other in spite of our feelings and differences from time to time. Because of our deep love for each, I declare that in our union, divorce or separation is not an option. We will uphold each other in love no matter what happens. The two of us are better than one of us. We are bigger, richer, stronger, safer and better together as one than apart.

Lord Jesus, I love my partner with an unconditional love. My love for my partner covers all my partner's lapses, shortcomings, weaknesses and sins. So no matter what my partner does or does not, I love my partner. Even when my partner fails or falls or fumbles, I will love my partner till death do us part. I love my partner to help my partner get back up when my partner falls or fails or fumbles. This is my prayer and declaration in the precious name of Jesus Christ my Lord and Master.

MY DREAM OF MY PARTNER

Take time to make a note of what you want your partner to look like. Your fantasies, expectations and desires.

WHY I CHOSE JESUS CHRIST?

Someone asked me many years ago, Mike, why did you accept Jesus Christ? I could have become an atheist, a Muslim, etc. Why Jesus Christ?

My answer to that question is for basically three reasons and the fourth one will blow your mind.

One, I accepted Jesus Christ because I needed a Father. A father is a life source. That means you came from him. According to the law of sustenance, you can only be sustained by your source. Fish came out of water and thus can only be sustained in a water environment. If you put it on land, no matter how nice looking, it will die in no distant time. I realized that God is my Source. I can only be sustained by Him. I discovered that I couldn't have a personal relationship with Him through any other one or way except through Jesus Christ. John 14:6. Acts 4:12.

Like a fish out of water in a land environment, you and I continue to struggle to survive until we reconnect with our natural habitat or source. This is God your Father. This happens only through Jesus Christ. You will never be fulfilled or become eternally relevant until you accept Jesus Christ into your heart as your personal Lord and Master. Then will you be able to connect with God your Source. Then will you know what it means to be sustained by the grace of God.

Two, I accepted Jesus Christ because I needed a friend. Man was designed to relate with his environment and people. Nobody can survive as an island. You will need friends in your life. For me, it is very easy to make friends. As I grew up, my life became messed up by the friends I had. Friends betrayed me. Some battered me. Yet some others left me each time after our relationship with bruises. The marks will always be there. It was my search unknown to me for the real friend that got me into such relationships. I did not know about the Friend that sticks closer than a brother. Proverbs 18:24.

Friends have scorned me like they did Job. Job's friends turned aside from him (Job 6:18). They laughed him to scorn (Job 12:4). He was such a laughing stock that his eyes poured out tears to God (Job 16:20). His kinfolks failed him. His friends forgot him (Job 19:14). I have been there.

I needed a friend who will love me the way I am. I found this Friend in Jesus. He is God who became Abraham's Friend (Gen. 18:17. 2 Chron. 20:7). What a Friend He was to Abraham that even when Abraham lied about his wife, God rebuked the king to restore Abraham's wife (Gen. 12:10-20. 20:1-18.). A true friend will be there for you in good times and bad ones. Jesus is the best Friend I have ever had in my life (John 15:14).

You will never know a true friend outside of Jesus Christ. Your parents? Spouse? Relatives? Classmates?

Colleagues? I choose Jesus Christ because He will be there for me all the time. He said so and I believe Him.

Three, I needed a future. Life is past, present and future. I have seen the past, it was both good and bad. I cannot do anything about it. It is gone forever. I failed in the past. I did all the bad things in the past. But it is gone leaving me with the consequences of my wrong choices and deeds. Now I am in the present. What can I do to make the difference for my future? This is what I am concerned with today. I discovered that it is only in Jesus Christ that His precious blood washes my past away. My today is secured with His ever-abiding presence because He is a very present help. My tomorrow is taken care of because He told me not to worry about it.

I have a beautiful future in Jesus Christ because of what He did for me at the cross. I sinned and deserved to die. He took my sins and died in my place. In exchange, He gave me His very life, abundant life.

The fourth reason is that He changed my life. Religion tries to change people by principles, philosophies and practices. But Jesus came into my life without Him putting any demands on me to do things to earn His forgiveness. All He asked from me was to believe and receive Him. I did and found that my life is just changing every day. When I started this journey, I did not look like what I am today. I am not the same every day. I can assure you that by tomorrow I will become better. Until the day when I shall be changed permanently at the sound of the trump of God. From that point, I will put on immortality and incorruption. Sin shall never have dominion over me for all eternity. Is this not the kind of life you really desire from the deepest part of your being?

Today, my friend, you must make up your mind to receive Jesus Christ or reject Him. It is your choice. If you want to choose Jesus Christ, it is easy. Just say out loud:

Jesus, I believe you came to this world because You love me. Your love constrained You to the cross where You died for my sins to be forgiven me. Jesus, I believe. Come into my heart today. Wash me with Your precious blood. Make me a new person whose love and passion will be for You the rest of my life on earth. Jesus, You are the Lord of my life from this day forward. Thank You for saving me in Jesus name. Amen.

If you have prayed this prayer, do write me today and I will send you some materials to help you in this journey to become all that God has designed you to be.

PARTNER WITH US

When God gives one man a vision, it will require the participation of several others to fulfill that vision. No single individual can carry out God's vision because God gives according to His size. Anyone who tries to fulfill God's vision by themselves either will get frustrated or finished off. In 1989, God told Brother Mike, *'Son, take this gospel and miracle power of the living Christ to the nations – impacting lives and destinies with the WORD.'* Since then, that word has been the driving force to reaching 30 million souls in at least 50 nations.

"And they beckoned unto their partners, which were in the other ship, that they should come and help them. And they came, and filled both the ships, so that they began to sink." Luke 5:7.

Through this message, we are beckoning on you to come alongside with us through your support and partnership. Help us reach millions around the world. Help us to fill our boat with a massive harvest. The beauty of this partnership is that when you help us, our boat and your boat will be filled. Together, we shall have a net breaking and boat sinking harvest.

Three things you CAN do to help us:

1. You can PRAY. Zech. 10:1. Acts 4:28-30. Eph. 6:18-20. Your prayers travel faster than the speed of light. You can commit to pray for us on a regular basis.

2. You can PLANT your seed of any size. Your money or material seed is the mobile force that moves the gospel from person to person and place to place. Your money or material is YOU GOing places you may not have the chance to be physically. Give generously. You can give your offering and seeds with your credit or debit card with this email address: ***amamieye@yahoo.co.uk***   through

https://www.pay.google.com or MAWO account details:

GTBank account number 0038894924. If you are outside Nigeria, you can give through MoneyGram.com for free. GTBank accepts money through MoneyGram for free. Use it while the opportunity last.

In Nigeria, you can give by using your bank code as follows:

For offering, dial: *bankcode*000*491+amount#

For tithes, dial: *bankcode*000*492+amount#

If you are using GTBank for instance, your bank code is 737, so you can dial: *737*000*491+amount#

If you are in the United States of America, you can give your offering to Bank of America account number 0905418443. ABA Routing number is: 121000358.

With Zelle, send to: **amamieye@yahoo.co.uk**

If you are in the United Kingdom, you can give your offering to NatWest Bank account number 52344819. Sort code 602112.

3. You can PARTICIPATE with us as you join forces with us in any location near you. I look forward to see you as we gather together a net breaking and boat sinking harvest. Luke 5:7. If you hear a voice saying, ignore this message, just know that it is the old serpent from the Garden. Tell that voice to shut up because you are the sheep of Jesus and you only obey the voice of your Master Jesus Christ. John 10:27. Thank you very much for obeying His voice in your heart and for being a part of what God is doing with us around the nations.

FOR MORE INFORMATION

Send in your testimonies to let us know how this devotional has been a blessing to you.

Send in your prayer requests as well.

Stand with us to help us reach thirty million souls in fifty nations.

For more spiritual help, counseling and prayer ministration, contact:

Bishop Michael O. Amamieye
Michael Amamieye Word Outreach, International

a/k/a Aggressive Faith Ministries
Plot 13 Walter Akpana Lay Out off 394 Ikwerre
Road, Mile 5 Rumueprikom, P. O. Box 12378, Port
Harcourt, Nigeria.

Hotlines: +234901800MAWO, +2348050987377
WhatsApp: +2348036732188
U.S.A: +19162456157
www.aggressivefaith.org
E-mail: info@aggressivefaith.org

ABOUT THE AUTHOR

Psalm 40:2,3 is a keynote to the life and ministry of Michael O. Amamieye. He was radically saved, healed and delivered from the power of darkness that endangered his youth. He is a living proof of God's matchless and abundant grace.

Since 1983, Brother Mike has been president, pastor and pioneer of several fellowships, churches and movements. He is instrumental in birthing many sons and daughters unto glory. He is a consecrated bishop with an oversight that reaches five continents.

In 1984, the Lord called Brother Mike to world evangelism with a mandate to *take the gospel and miracle power of the risen Christ to the nations – impacting lives and destinies with the WORD!* He is the President of **Michael Amamieye Word Outreach International** *also known as* **Aggressive Faith Ministries** with headquarters in the Garden City of Port Harcourt, Nigeria. He is the President of **Intensive Ministers Training School**. He is the Chairman of **Aggressive Faith Publishing Company**. Through this ministry, Brother Mike is determined to reach at least thirty million souls in at least fifty nations with the simple proclamation of the gospel of Christ with evidence that brings salvation, healing, deliverance, blessing and joy.

An evangelist by calling, he is a graduate of the **Billy Graham School of Evangelism**. He is a member of **Proclamation Evangelism Network** and an associate evangelist with the **Global Network of Evangelists** founded by the **Luis Palau Association**. He has been interviewed on **Decision Today** Radio broadcast and **Decision** magazine both of which are owned by the **Billy Graham Evangelistic Association.** He has also appeared on GODTV as well as several other networks around the world.

Bishop Mike is a member of the **International Communion of Charismatic Churches** founded by the late Archbishop Benson Idahosa and several others. He has been honored in a public ceremony where the Mayor of the city of East Cleveland, Ohio gave him the key to the city in 2003. **LEADS Africa** honored him as an icon of nation building in 2012. **The Voice** magazine in Holland honored him with the spiritual leadership award in 2014. In 2019, he was awarded an honorary doctorate degree by **Triune Biblical University** in New York. He is on high demand in crusades, conferences and conventions around the world.

He is the author of more than twenty books. He is a prolific and thought captivating writer with many of his works published in newsletters, magazines and newspapers around the world.

Bishop Mike is happily married to Princess Monivi, an ordained minister of the gospel and a health consultant. They are blessed with two biological children, Edwina Aleme and Mehetabel Favour as well as many others.

Welcome To The Partner Family

"They signaled to their partners in other boat to come and take hold with them. And they came and filled both the boats, so that they began to sink." Luke 5:7. (Amplified Version).

Since the Lord gave me the vision of a massive harvest of souls through the mandate to reach 30 million souls for whom Christ died in at least 50 countries, I have not ceased to signal my partners *to come and take hold with me*.

Through our mass evangelistic crusades, we are seeing many become born again. It is amazing as God is giving us the gates of our enemies. We are seeing hardened criminals, cult leaders, gang leaders, etc, become born again.

This is possible because of the sacrifices of committed partners who have responded to our calls.

Now, it is your turn to respond to my signal. I want to give you an opportunity to fill your boat with miracles until it begins to sink.

Please check appropriate boxes:

☐ **I WANT TO BECOME A MONTHLY PARTNER.** I am expecting my partner information packet with more details. My offering is enclosed to start my partnership. I am willing to commit monthly: ☐ **$15** ☐ **$20** ☐ **$25** ☐ **$50** ☐ **$100**

☐ **I WANT TO HELP SPONSOR A CRUSADE.** Enclosed is my special one-time gift of: ☐ **$1000** ☐ **$2000** ☐ **$3000** ☐ **$__________**

**Tear this form and send to us with your prayer requests.
Use the address you find in this book.**